MW01675765

Tip of the Iceberg

A Book About the Clitoris

Tip of the

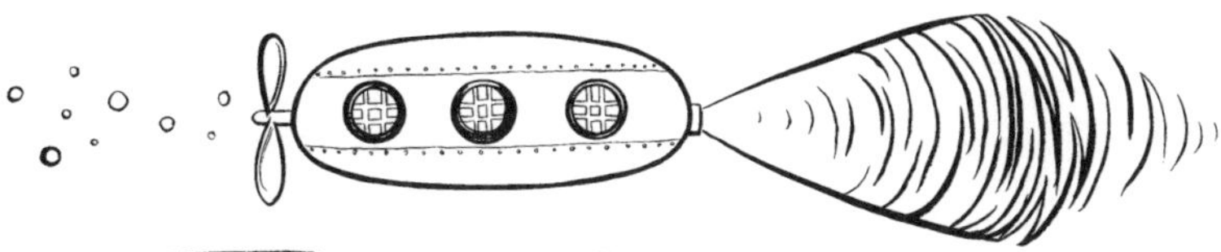

Iceberg

A Book About the Clitoris

Written & illustrated by

Laura Szumowski

For my parents, and all the Peter Mayle books they shared with me.

Tip of the Iceberg: A Book About the Clitoris

ISBN 978-0-9828224-4-9

LCCN 2012938975

Published by ZMK Press
www.zmkpress.com

Printed in Michigan.

Special thanks to all of the people who offered their input, feedback and grammatical expertise.

Image reference for pages 28-30 used with permission from Suzann Gage and The Federation of Feminist Women's Health Centers.

Table of Contents

The clitoris is like an iceberg; only the tip is visible on the outside, its larger mass is...

under the surface.

—Jennifer Johnson, "*Exposed at Last: The Truth About Your Clitoris*"

PopQuiz

the clitoris

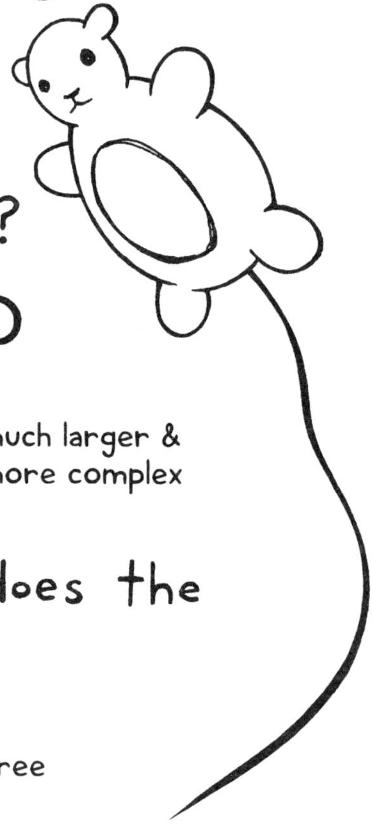

1 How big is yours?

A.) 

B.) 

C.) 

D.) much larger & more complex

2 How many parts does the clitoris have?

A.) one

B.) three

C.) more than ten

D.) the clitoris has parts?

3 What happens to the clitoris when you (& it) become aroused?

A.) you have an erection

B.) nothing

C.) it sends telepathic messages to your partner

D.) you have to pee

4 How do you find your G-Spot?

A.) it's a myth

B.) under a blacklight

C.) with your fingers

D.) with a speculum

5 Where does orgasm come from?

A.) vagina

B.) clitoris

C.) g-spot

D.) what orgasm?

Answers located in the following pages →

fun facts!

Q: How is it pronounced?

A: There are two ways: "KLIT-or-iss" or "kli-TOR-iss."

➩ The word "clitoris" comes from the Greek verb *kleitoriazein* meaning "to titillate."

➩ In German, *Kitzler* is a term for the clitoris meaning "tickler."

➩ Or *Wollustkorperchen* for "corpuscles of sexual pleasure."

Parts of the Clitoris

There are two kinds of parts to the clitoris: some are on the OUTSIDE, where you can see and feel them. However, the main body of the clitoris is found on the INSIDE, hidden from view.

sponges

lips

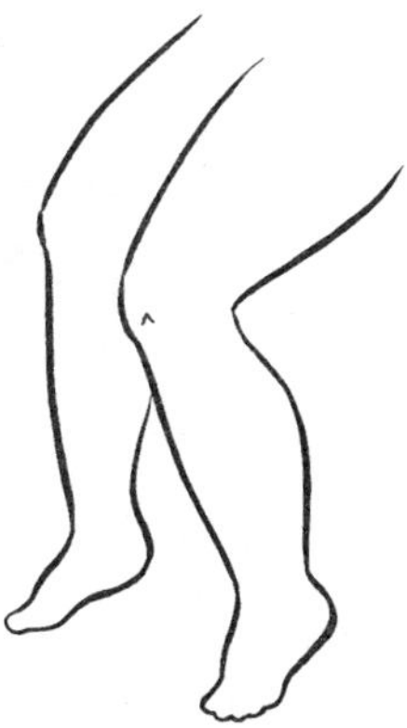

legs

bulbs

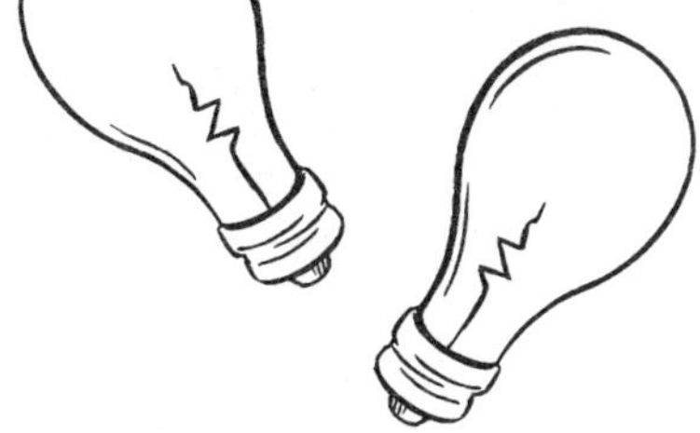

the Visible parts

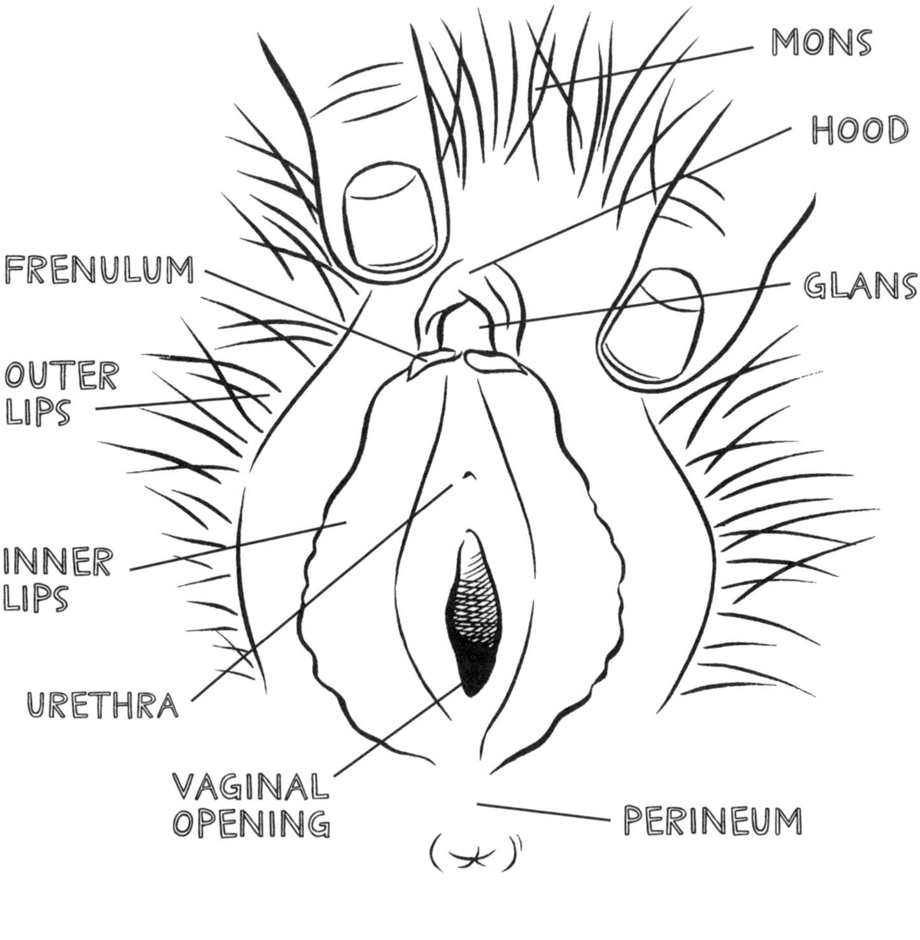

TIP: The glans has about 8,000 nerve endings (so it tends to get most of the attention), but it's only a small portion of the clitoris.

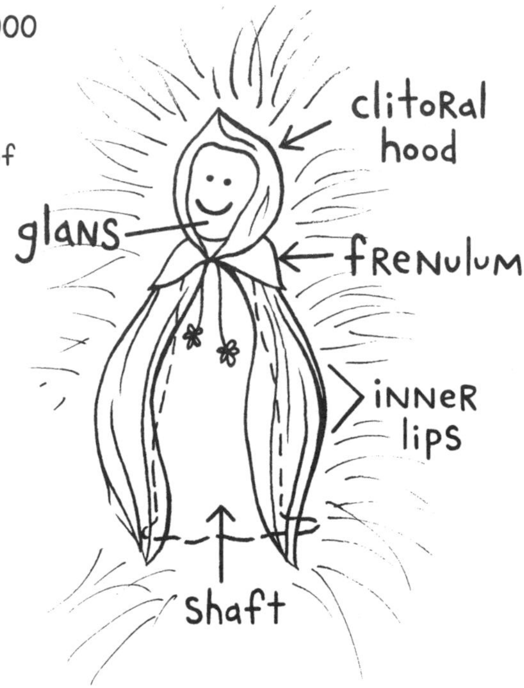

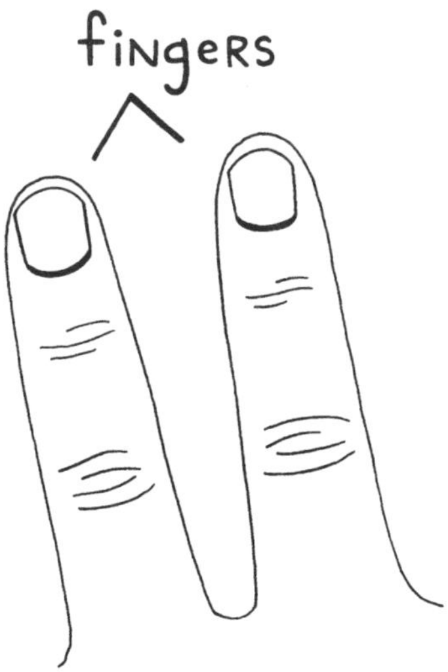

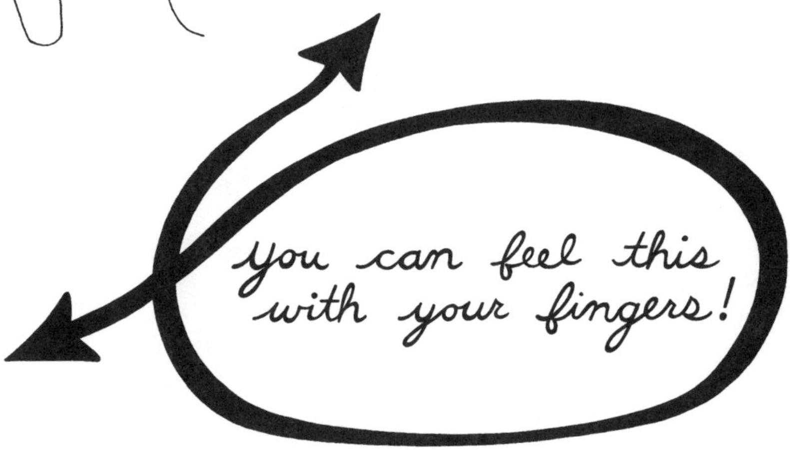

the Less Visible Parts

The majority of your clitoris is inside your body. The main parts of the internal clitoris are: two corpora cavernosa, two crura, and two bulbs.

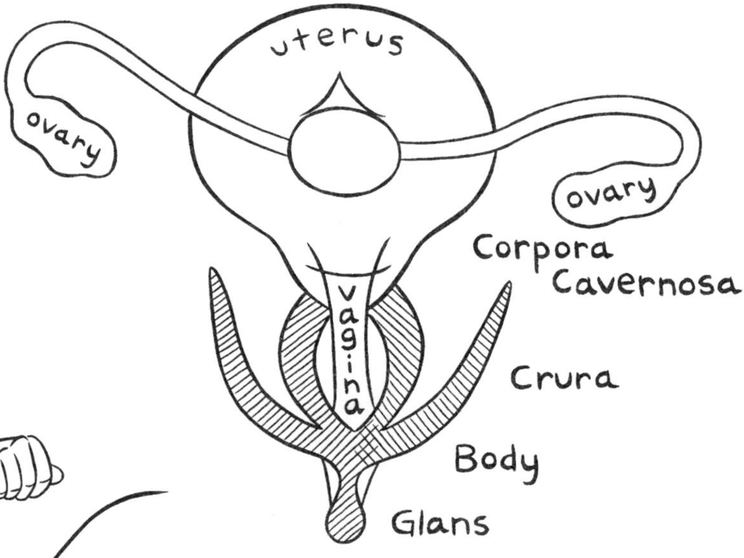

Muscles

At orgasm, the muscles surrounding the vagina and clitoris play a major role. As they contract, the erectile tissues and sensitive nerve endings are compressed (creating a very pleasurable sensation).

Erectile Tissue

There are two types of erectile tissue in the clitoris: one FIRM, one ELASTIC. During sexual excitement, they fill with blood and become firmer, supporting erection.

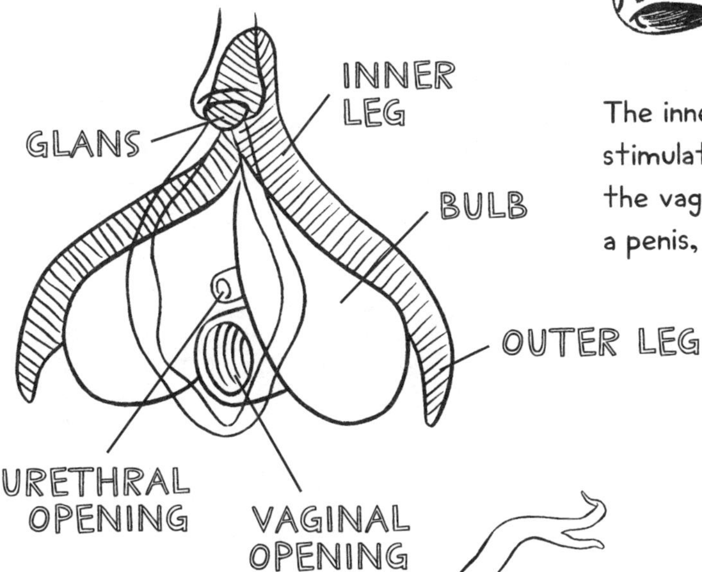

The inner clitoris can be stimulated by exploring the vagina with fingers, a penis, or a toy.

Since it's below the surface, the inner clitoris is better suited to pressure and massage (rather than a lighter touch usually enjoyed by the glans).

fun facts!

In case you were wondering...

The size of your clitoris has no effect on the intensity of your orgasms or sexual response.

When aroused, the glans swells to twice its usual size.

cli·to·ris *noun*
plural cli·to·ris·es also cli·to·ri·des
[Origin: early 17th century: modern Latin, from Greek *kleitoris*]
: a small sensitive and erectile organ at the anterior end of the vulva.

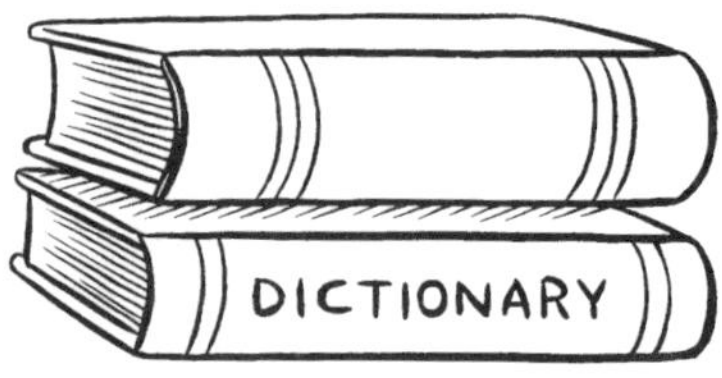

an ENCYCLOPEDIA of parts!

THE ANATOMY OF THE CLITORIS

Thought the clitoris was simple? Think again! While you can't see most of it, your clitoris is a complex structure with a variety of parts. Don't worry, you won't need to keep track of every detail – your clitoris knows what it's doing.

OF NOTE:

⇨ The parts on pages 18+19 are external and visible. Grab a mirror and see them for yourself!

⇨ The parts on pages 20–23 make up the internal structure of the clitoris, and are therefore not visible. (Exception: the vaginal opening, which is easy to see.)

⇨ All of the parts are presented in order of appearance from the top (sort of). If you get lost, try cross-referencing with the illustration on page 24.

VULVA

People sometimes confuse the vulva with the vagina. "Vagina" refers to the canal inside the body, while the "vulva" consists of several parts that can be seen on the outside of the body (the mons and two pairs of lips).

OUTER LIPS

There are two sets of lips – you can tell which ones are your outer lips because they have hair. (a.k.a. labia majora.)

INNER LIPS

Between the outer lips, you'll find two folds of sensitive skin – these are the inner lips (a.k.a. labia minora). Spread them to see the external parts of the clitoris, along with the vaginal opening.

FRONT COMMISURE

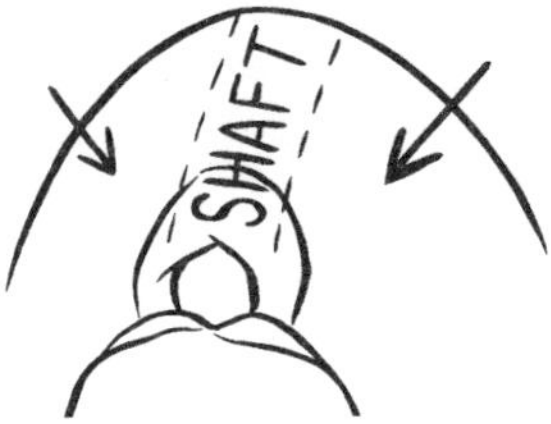

It's a name you might not hear very often, but this is the part directly above the hood. Massaging this spot is a great way to stimulate the shaft of the clitoris.

HOOD

Like a tent, the hood is formed where the inner lips meet over the glans and shaft. It connects to the glans and protects it from overexposure, and is similar to the foreskin of a penis.

GLANS

If you pull back the hood, you'll find the glans (a.k.a clit). This is the "tip" of the clitoris – the most sensitive part of the entire genital area. It has roughly 8,000 nerve endings, more than anywhere else in the human body!

SHAFT

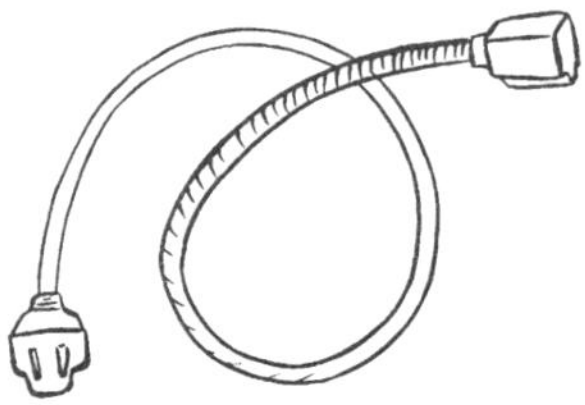

Attached to the glans is a firm, rubbery cord that moves when you press it. The shaft connects to the pubic bone and internal clitoris, and pushes the glans forward during arousal.

INNER LEGS

Connected to the shaft are two pieces of erectile tissue called the inner legs, or corpora cavernosa. When erect, they wrap around the vagina and may be stimulated internally.

OUTER LEGS

The inner legs divide into two long, thin bands of erectile tissue that flare out and run along the pubic bone, forming a wishbone shape. (a.k.a. crura.)

BULBS

Near each of the legs is another type of erectile tissue called the bulbs (a.k.a. clitoral vestibules). On either side of the vaginal opening and underneath the outer lips, the bulbs fill with blood during arousal, causing the vulva and vaginal opening to change shape.

URETHRA

A.k.a. where pee comes out. A short tube that leads to the bladder. This may be difficult to see or locate with your hands.

URETHRAL SPONGE

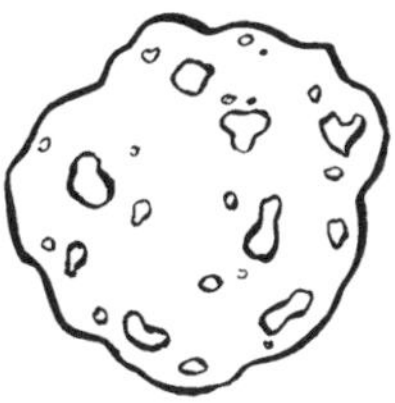

A pad of soft erectile tissue that extends inward along the ceiling of the vagina. It surrounds the urethra, protecting it from pressure and the entry of bacteria during sexual activity. The urethral sponge is part of the G-spot! Learn more on page 33.

G-SPOT

An area on the anterior (front) wall of the vagina that may be sensitive and swells when stimulated. This is more of an area than a spot, and contains the urethral sponge and prostate. See page 33 for more info.

PROSTATE

Also called the Skene's Glands, the female prostate is a set of glands that swell with blood during arousal and secrete lubrication when stimulated. Located between the vaginal wall and urethra, the prostate is linked with female ejaculation. See pages 33–35.

VAGINAL OPENING

Found below the urethral opening, it is an elastic opening formed by closely folded skin.

HYMEN

A smooth ring of tissue that surrounds the vaginal opening, about one inch inside the vagina. Once you've had vaginal intercourse, the hymen remains as small petal-like bits of tissue.

VAGINAL CANAL

The pathway for menstrual fluid, tampons, menstrual cups, speculums, fingers, dildos, penises, or babies at birth. Also known as the "birth canal," the vagina is composed of expandable tissue and muscle.

PERINEUM

That spot between your vagina and butt hole (or anus). It does a couple things: one, it stretches (a lot) at childbirth; two, it covers the "perineal body" – three pairs of muscles that contract in unison during orgasm.

PERINEAL SPONGE

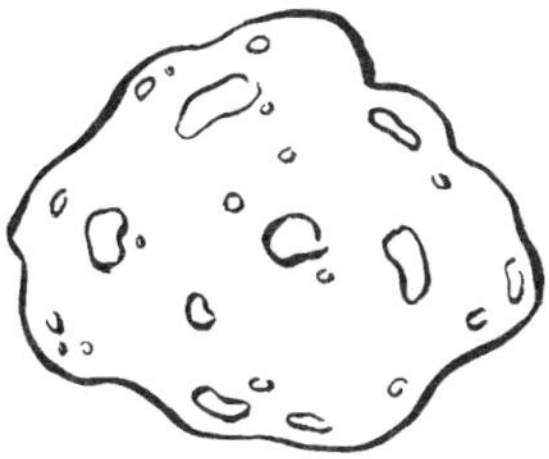

A spongy cushion composed of erectile tissue and blood vessels. During arousal, it swells with blood and compresses the outer third of the vagina along with the tissues of the clitoris.

PELVIC DIAPHRAGM

A voluntary muscle attached to the pelvic bones and wrapped around the rectum and vagina. All the structures of the clitoris rest on this large muscle, which tightens the rectum and vagina when contracted. You can strengthen your pelvic diaphragm with Kegel exercises! See page 36.

The Clitoris at Rest

This is a view of the clitoris when it's relaxed and unaroused.

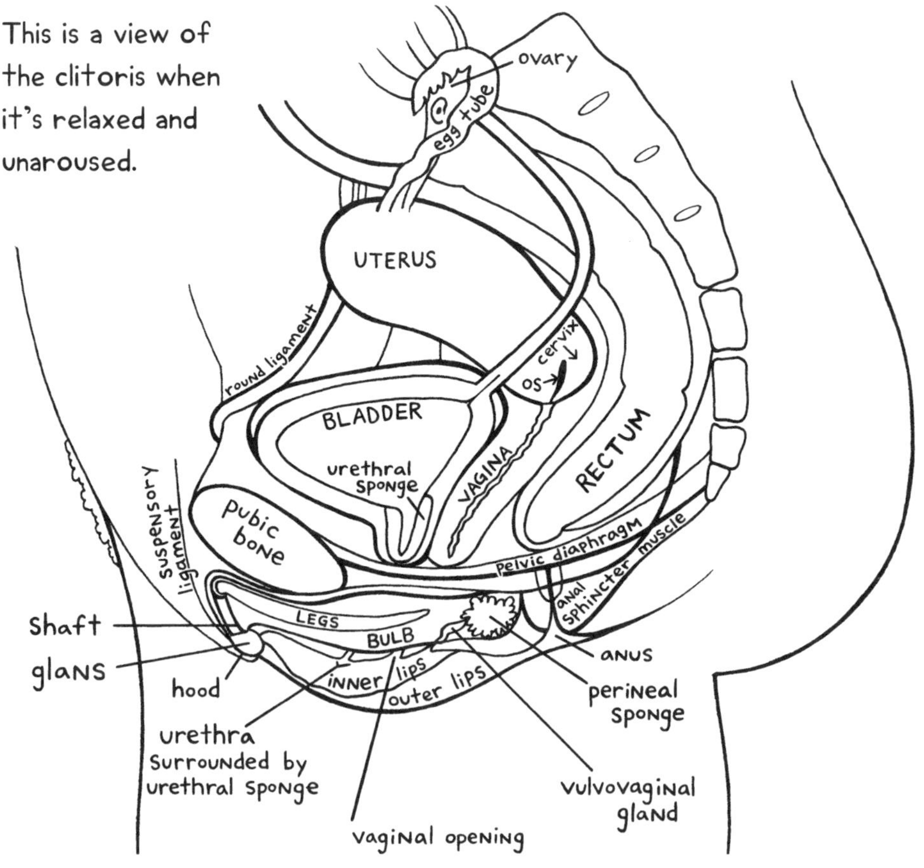

erection

The Clitoris in its Erect State

Here's what goes on with the clitoris (and its neighboring parts) during erection.

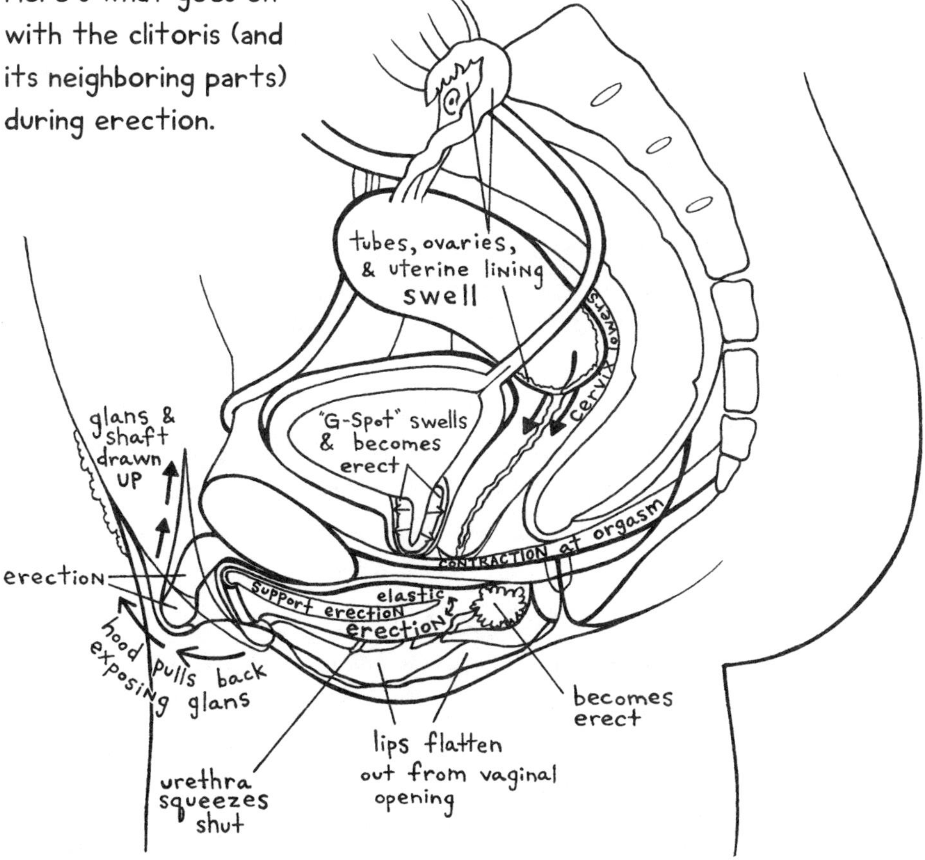

fun facts!

Q: What makes multiple orgasms possible?

A: As it swells with blood during arousal, the clitoris stays at ease. (This makes it different from a penis, which becomes rigid due to special blood vessels that keep blood trapped inside it during erection.) In the clitoris, blood can flow in and out, and it can swell and relax easily – this allows for multiple orgasms.

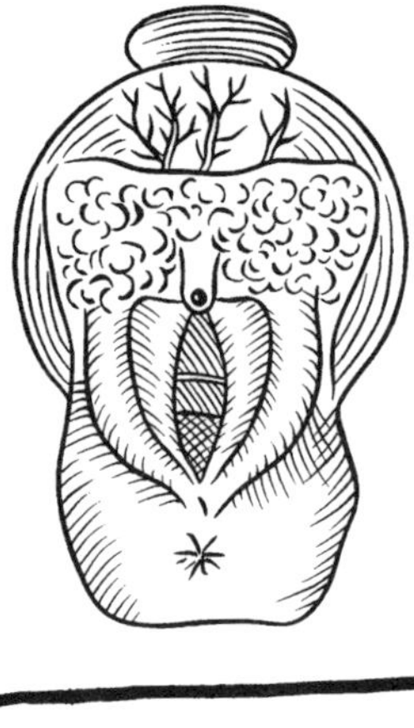

The earliest picture of the external genitalia was drawn by anatomist Severinus Pineus (1550–1619).

(It's hard to tell whether this illustration is missing the clitoris or the urethra.)

The Stages of Sexual Response

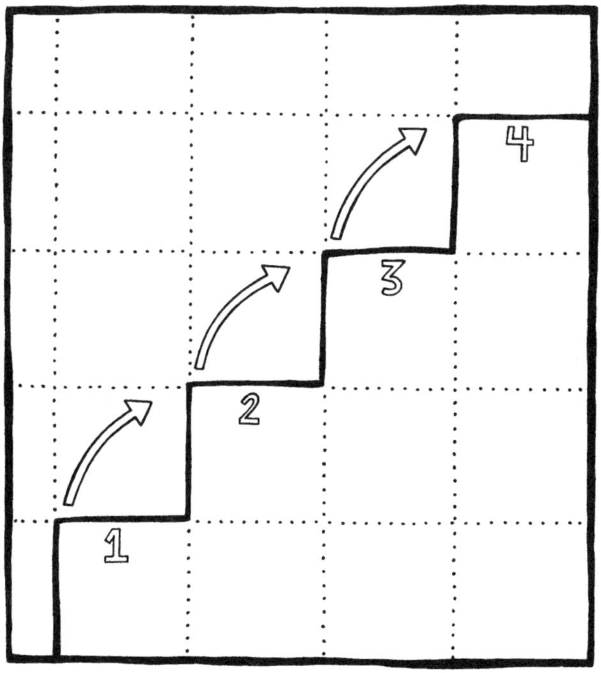

These are the basic steps of sexual response – but sex doesn't always go "by-the-book." For example, you may experience a nice back and forth between excitement and plateau, multiple orgasms before resolution, and other variations. Any way you hack it, the first step is desire.

This is an inner view of the non-erect clitoris.

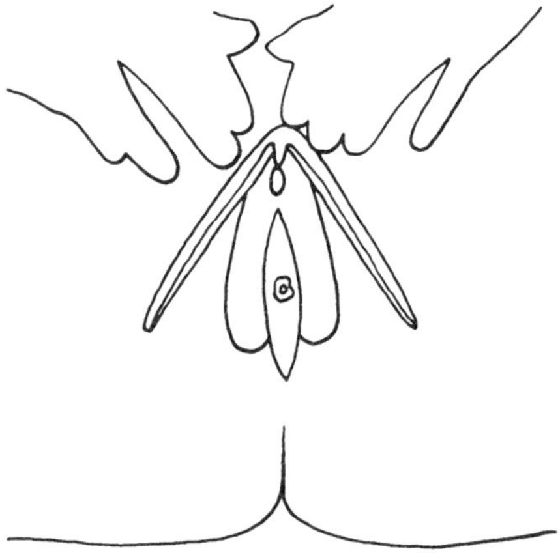

Stage 1: DESIRE

When you feel the desire for a sexual encounter (with yourself or a partner).

Stage 2: EXCITEMENT

The clitoris becomes erect, filling with blood.

- outer labia lay flat, while the inner labia swell & darken
- vagina begins to lubricate
- uterus starts moving up and away from the vagina
- clitoris becomes extra-sensitive

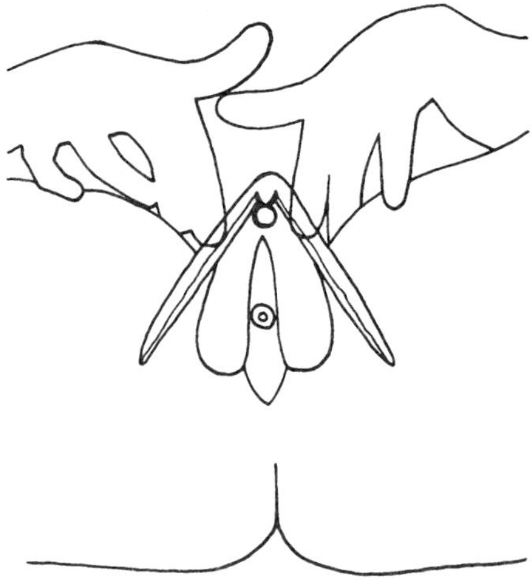

Stage 3: PLATEAU

(OR: EXCITEMENT PART TWO)

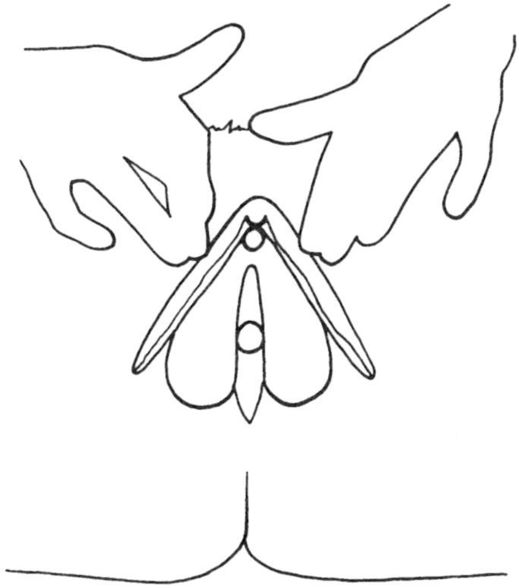

Everything swells as blood flow continues to increase.

- outer third of the vaginal wall thickens and contracts
- clitoris pulls back under its hood
- heart rate and blood pressure increase
- skin begins to flush

Stage 4: ORGASM

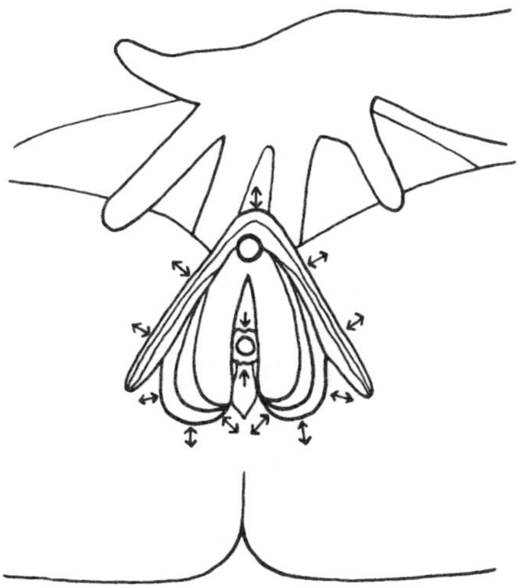

Powerful muscle contractions in the clitoris, vagina, uterus and lower pelvic muscles.

- muscles tense
- breathing, heart rate, and blood pressure rise further
- ejaculation may occur

The clitoral muscles as they contract during orgasm.

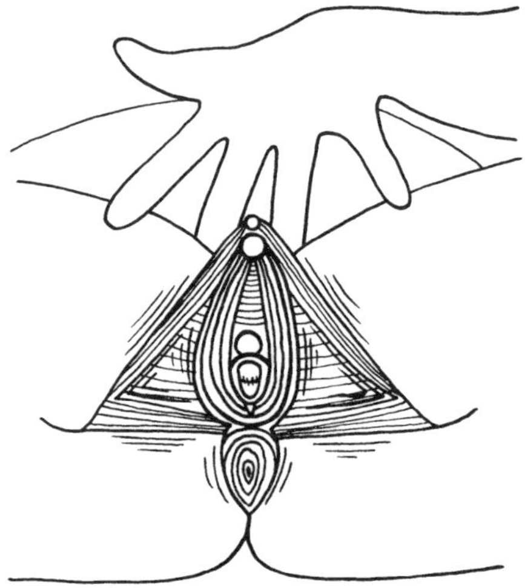

Stage 5: RESOLUTION

Blood no longer floods the clitoris. Tissues shrink and the pulse slows.

- labia and vaginal walls gradually return to their resting state
- breathing and blood pressure return to normal
- muscles relax

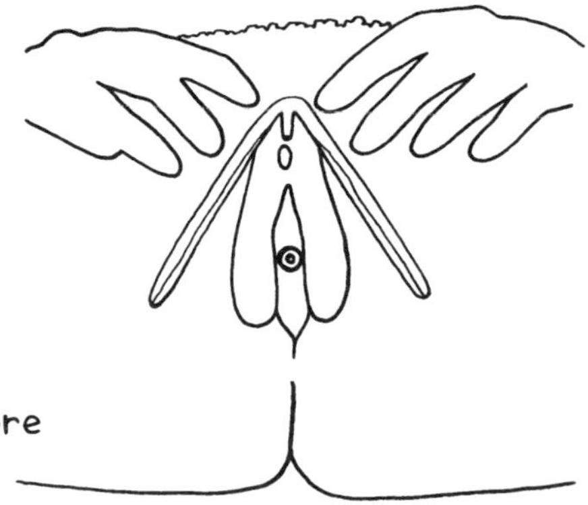

NOTE: If stimulation continues, it can delay or stop resolution, and more orgasms can happen.

Just the Facts!

The Uterus and such

During sexual arousal, the lining of the uterus becomes swollen with blood, and it balloons upward, enlarging the vagina.

At the same time, the fallopian tubes and ovaries swell.

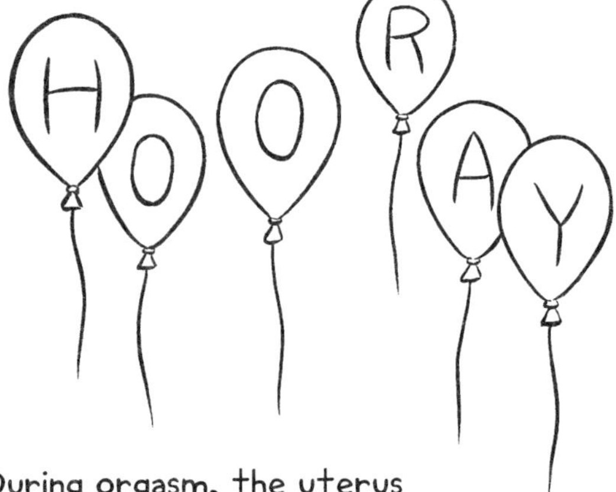

CERVIX

During orgasm, the uterus contracts rhythmically.

The neck of the cervix is flexible, like an accordion. During orgasm, the cervix opens slightly and moves forward and down, dipping into the seminal pool (that is, the cum) if a partner has ejaculated.

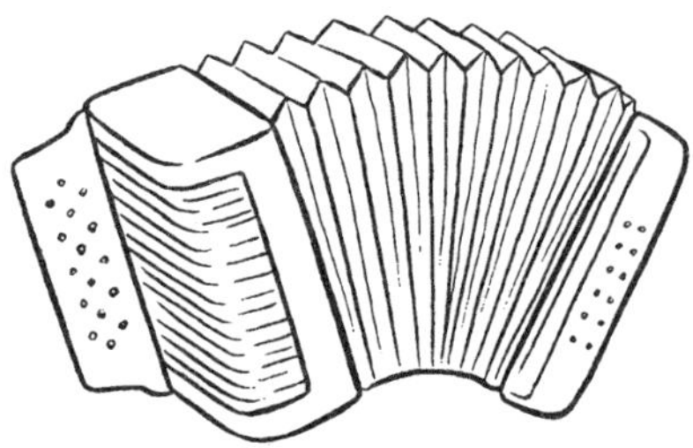

THE G Spot

The g-spot is a bean-shaped area about a finger's length inside the vagina. The name 'g-spot' is a bit of a misnomer: it's more of a zone than a self-contained spot. When this area is stimulated, the urethral sponge and female prostate are also involved.

You can feel the g-spot by inserting a finger or two into your vagina and pressing up toward your pubic bone (the front of your body). A "come hither" finger motion will stimulate the g-spot, which can be pleasurable for many folks. Stimulating this area may make you feel like you have to pee, a sensation similar to the urge to ejaculate.

FUN FACT:

Sensations from the clitoris and g-spot travel along different nerves to the brain, so their orgasms feel different too.

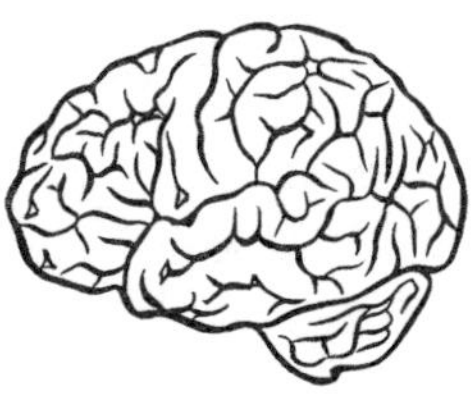

When it is stroked, it will puff out and feel like a marshmallow.

WHAT is Female EJACULATION?

Ejaculation: the release of fluid from the urethra at orgasm.

Where does it come from?

The female prostate (also called the paraurethral glands) is a set of glands found in the same area as the g-spot. During arousal, and when stimulated, these glands produce a fluid.

But isn't ejaculation the same as peeing?

Nope. Ejaculate is a mixture of prostatic fluid, glucose, and trace amounts of urine. It's usually a clear fluid, but it can also appear milky or creamy. Ejaculate has a variety of tastes and smells, but it doesn't look or smell like pee.

Do YOU ejaculate?

You may or may not, and you might without even noticing it. The amount of ejaculate can vary from a tablespoon to a cup or two (or none at all).

How does it happen?

The glands of the prostate open into the urethra, so when muscles contract during orgasm it forces the prostatic fluid through the urethra and out of the body. Ejaculate does not come from the bladder.

Note:

The interesting thing about the female prostate is that it varies from person to person. In some cases, none of this glandular tissue is present at all. This explains the wide ranging experiences of ejaculation, and why some people can or can't.

FUN FACT: the Skene's gland was officially renamed "female prostate" in 2002 by the *Federative International Committee on Anatomical Terminology*. It is homologous* to the prostate gland in males.

*homologous means the same organ with a common structure.

Kegel exer-cises

WHAT: Strengthening of the pelvic diaphragm, also called the pelvic floor muscles or PC muscle.

WHY: The PC muscle contracts during orgasm, and also supports childbirth and urinary control. Excercising it can increase sexual pleasure and orgasm, ease childbirth, and help prevent problems controlling urine flow (incontinence).

WHERE: Anywhere: in a car, at work, at dinner, in bed, on the bus, on a date...

HOW: Contract your muscles as if you're trying to stop peeing, or tighten your vagina around one or two fingers. Tighten the muscles and hold for 2 to 4 seconds; relax for ten seconds. Repeat 5 times. Do this 3 times a day. Gradually work up to 8 second holds, repeated ten times. Then add 3 or 4 short, fast, strong twitches at the end of each long contraction.

THE CLITORIS THROUGHOUT HISTORY (in snapshots!)

Over time, the clitoris has gone in and out of fashion. Science and medicine left it unexplored for many years, while society ignored it in favor of the vagina's link with conception (and babies). Remember: increasing the population was once a much more valuable skill than it is today.

One of the greatest shifts took place in the 20th century, when Freud declared clitoral orgasm to be adolescent, and vaginal orgasm (without any clitoral stimulation) the proper response for healthy adults. The consequence: those who could not achieve orgasm through vaginal intercourse were labeled abnormal, unhealthy and frigid. On a more private level, people struggled to have satisfying sex lives within the confines of Freud's flawed (yet popular) philosophy.

Since then, many have disproved Freud's theory (Alfred Kinsey, Masters & Johnson, Shere Hite, among others) with years of scientific research and observation, revealing the true workings of the clitoris and human sexual function.

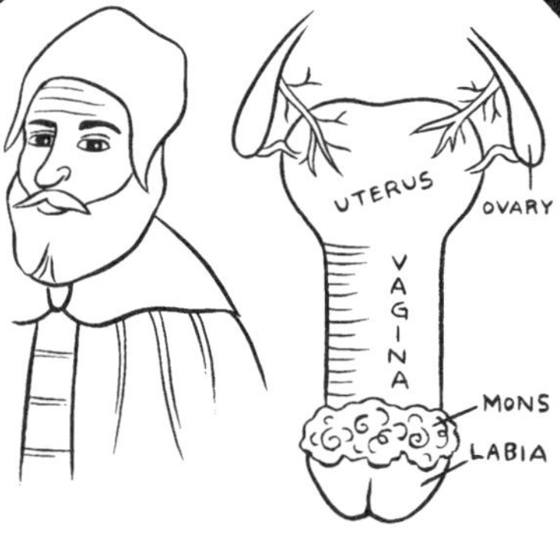

160 A.D. Claudius Galen establishes the one-sex model, describing female genitalia as an inversion of the penis.

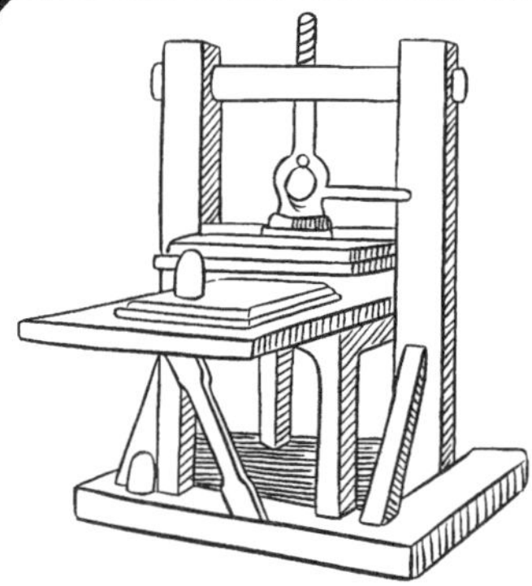

1436 Gutenberg invents the printing press, spreading information and ideas, especially among scientists.

1500s studies of anatomy recognize the role of the clitoris as a major part of sexual pleasure.

1559 Renaldus Columbus claims he has discovered the clitoris.

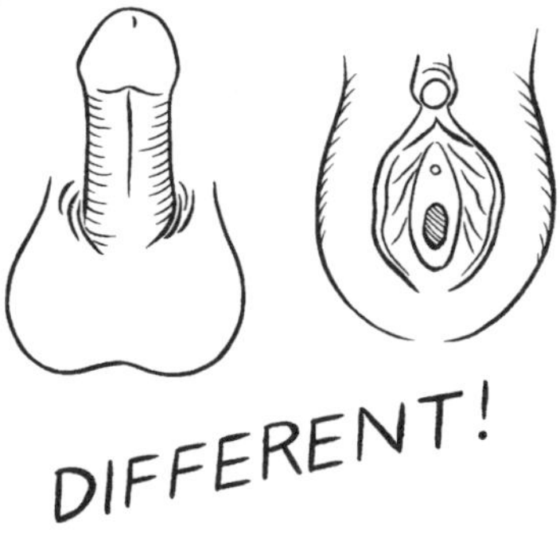

18th Century the one-sex is replaced by the two-sex model; female & male genitalia are direct opposites.

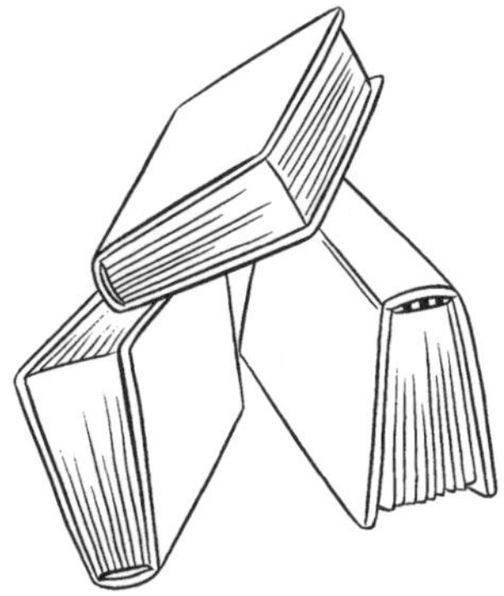

Late 1800s the print industry speeds up with the rotary press, making books much more affordable.

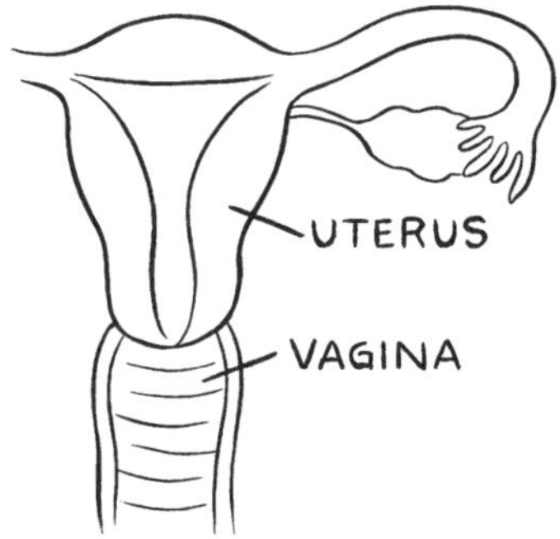

Early 1900s it finally becomes normal to distinguish the uterus from the vagina and vulva.

1905 physicians believe sewing machines, bicycles, and horseback riding lead to masturbation.

1905 Freud introduces his idea of two kinds of orgasm: clitoral (immature) and vaginal (mature).

1924 Princess Marie Bonaparte suggests the "Rule of Thirds": if the clitoris & vagina are more than a thumb's length apart, it may be difficult to reach orgasm (through intercourse).

By 1930 Freud's claim has become the dominant model of normal sexual function.

1948 & 1953 the Kinsey Reports are published. Alfred Kinsey interviews thousands of women and men about their sex lives.

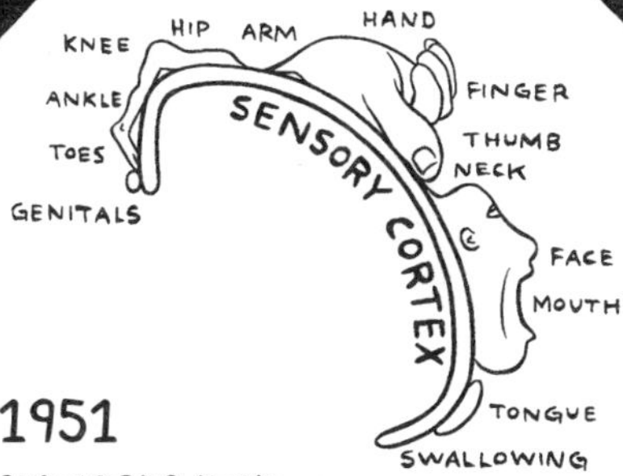

1951
surgeons map
the sensory cortex
(the connection between the brain & the body). However, all the subjects are male, leaving female genitalia unmapped.

1954 a group of Freud's peers insist that 80–90% of all women are sexually "abnormal."

1957–1965 Masters and Johnson test Kinsey's theories through direct observation in the laboratory.

1976 Shere Hite publishes The Hite Report on Female Sexuality, focusing on individual sexual experiences.

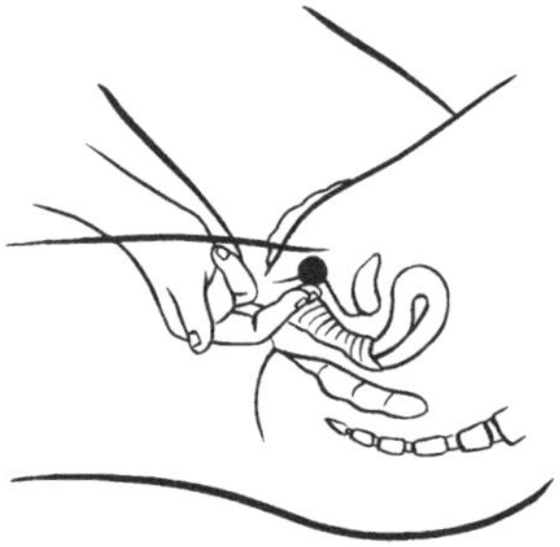

1982 the "G-Spot" is named after German gynecologist Ernst Grafenberg, and popularized by the book *The G Spot and Other Discoveries About Human Sexuality.*

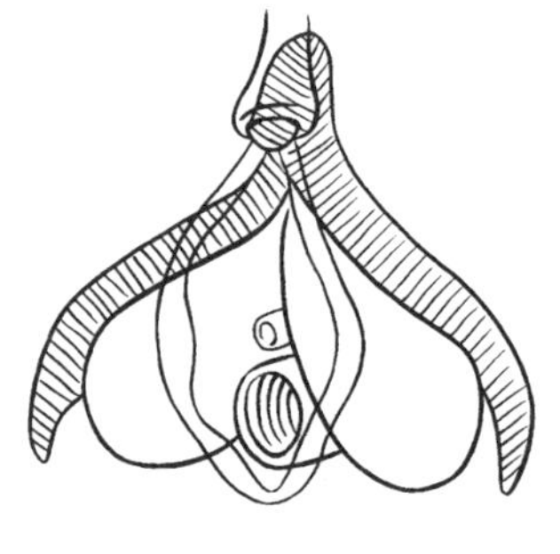

1998 urologist Helen O'Connell maps the internal structure of the excited clitoris using MRI, revealing the extent of its size.

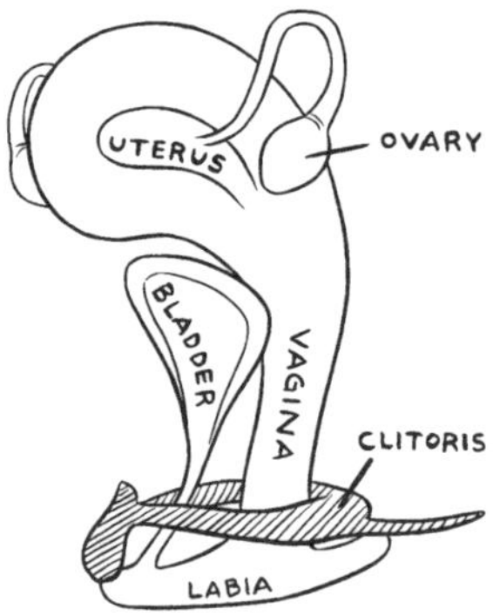

2009 French researchers produce the first 3D sonography of the stimulated clitoris & its erectile tissue.

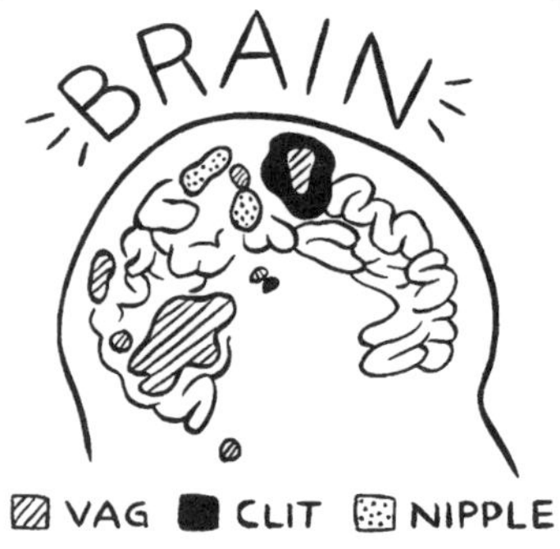

2010–2011 researchers use MRI to map the clitoris, cervix, vagina and nipples on the sensory cortex.

The *History* of the VIBRATOR

In Western medicine, "massage" has been used to treat a variety of ailments, but no ailment was more popular than hysteria. Until it was officially removed from the American Psychiatric Association's list of diseases in 1952, hysteria was one of the most frequently diagnosed disorders in history.

People have been engineering vibrators since the Medieval days (and earlier) for the same reasons we've created microwaves and bicycles: to get the job done faster and easier. A vibrator made a handy substitute for the time and labor of a skilled physician or massage therapist.

And yes, if you understand what the typical vibrator is used for today, you'll have a pretty good idea what doctors and nurses were doing *before* its invention. (Hint: the symptoms of hysteria were virtually the same as normal sexual function, and were typically treated with orgasm.)

"Ancient Times"

Vibrating parts of water-powered saws are used for massage by padding them with fabric.

manual massage

rocking chairs

Baths and bathing establishments offer water pressure and hand-held devices for stimulation.

Medieval (5th-15th century)

Before vibrators, physicians used manual massage, hydrotherapy, swings, rocking chairs, and gadgets that bounced patients on their pelvis.

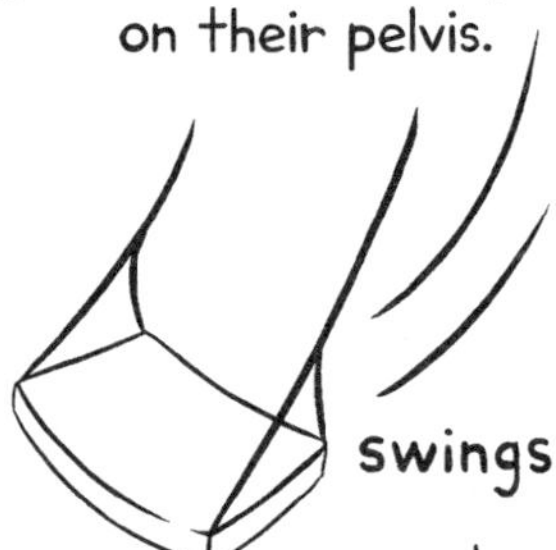

swings

Renaissance (14th-17th century)

Ancient Times!

Other Pre-Vibrator Devices

Bathing

Public opinion about bathing begins to change with the idea that frequent bathing might lead to better health.

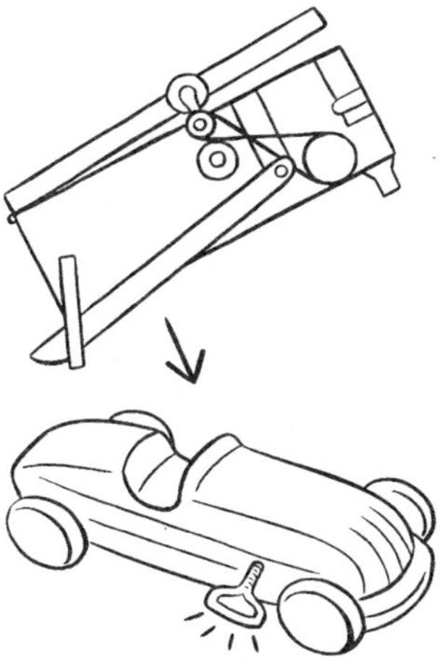

Trémoussoir

Abbe St. Pierre invents a wind-up vibrator. This is the world's FIRST vibrator!

The "Water Cure" becomes popular. Water is used to treat pain and illness with mineral baths, underwater massage, whirlpools and hot tubs.

The Water Cure

1734

Mid/Late 1700s

1830s

The Manipulator

A Steam powered vibrator (a padded table with a cut-out and vibrating parts) is patented by an American physician.

Unfortunately, doctors find this method inconvenient because they have to shovel coal into its boiler.

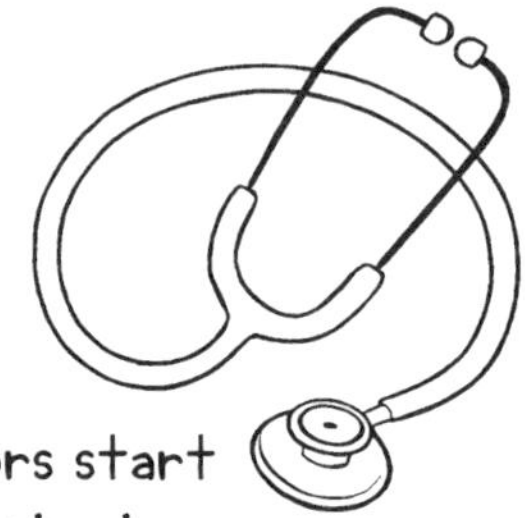

Vibrators start appearing in physicians' offices.

Note: these vibrators are powered by electricity, so they're not portable. You have to visit your doctor to use one.

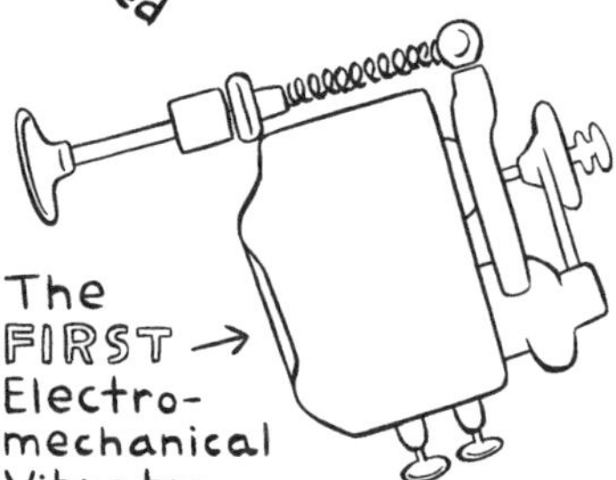

The first electromechanical vibrator is marketed to physicians.

3/4 of the female population is considered unhealthy or suffering from hysteria.

1869

1883

Late 1800s

WATER

Water starts becoming available in homes, thanks in part to the germ theory

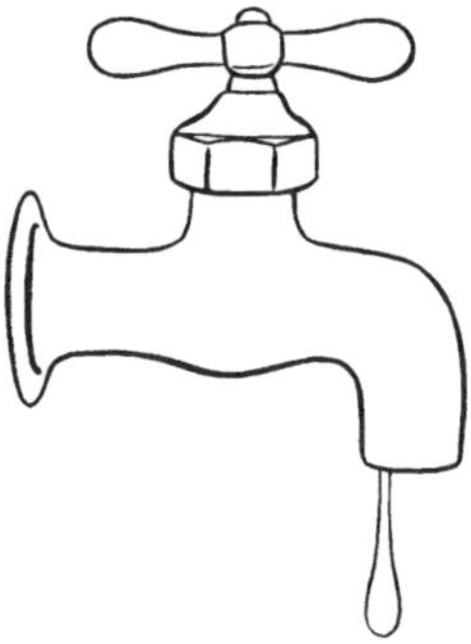

Germ Theory

(The theory that microorganisms cause disease.)

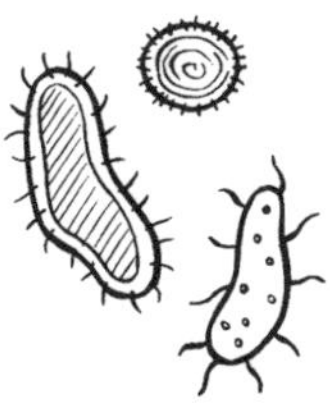

By the End of the 19th Century

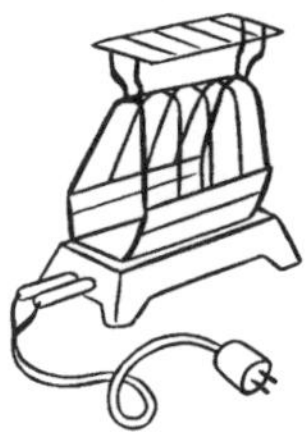

(5)

Hamilton Beach

Hamilton Beach patents the first electric vibrator. It's the fifth domestic appliance to be electrified, following the sewing machine, fan, tea kettle & toaster.

1902

Chattanooga

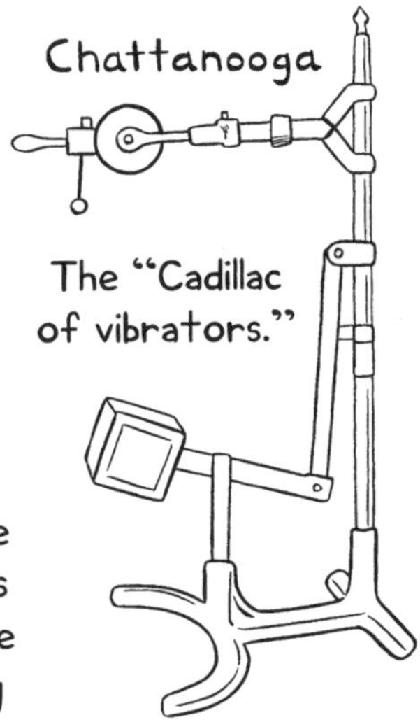

The "Cadillac of vibrators."

Cost $200 plus freight!

1904

House Calls

Vibrators become portable, allowing for house calls.

There are at least 10 vibrator manufacturers in the U.S.

Vibrators are marketed as a health and relaxation aid in magazines like Needlecraft and Modern Woman.

Sears, Roebuck & Co. advertises a home motor with a vibrator attachment (plus attachements for churning, mixing, grinding, buffing, beating, and running a fan).

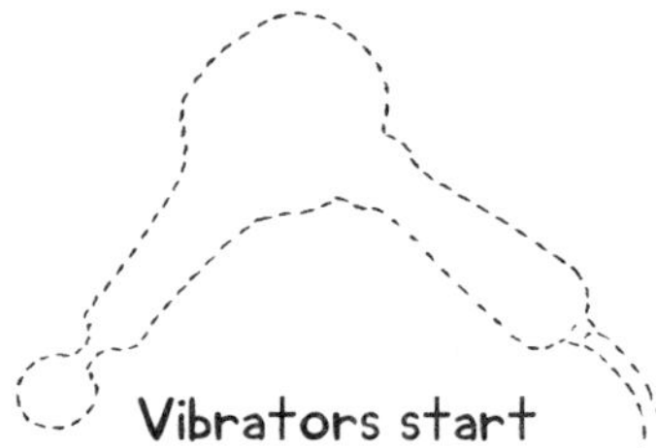

Vibrators start disappearing from magazines and doctors' offices, as a better understanding of sexuality develops (and vibrators begin showing up in porn).

1905 | 1918 | 1920ish | Late 20s

American Psychiatric Association

The American Psychiatric Association removes Hysteria from its list of diseases.

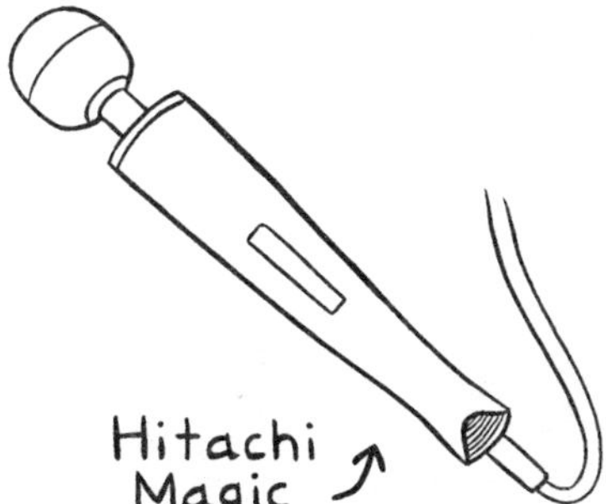

Hitachi Magic Wand

Vibrators re-emerge!

They are no longer considered medical instruments.

The cordless vibrator is patented in 1968.

Vibrators start being openly marketed as a sex aid.

1952

1960s

1970s

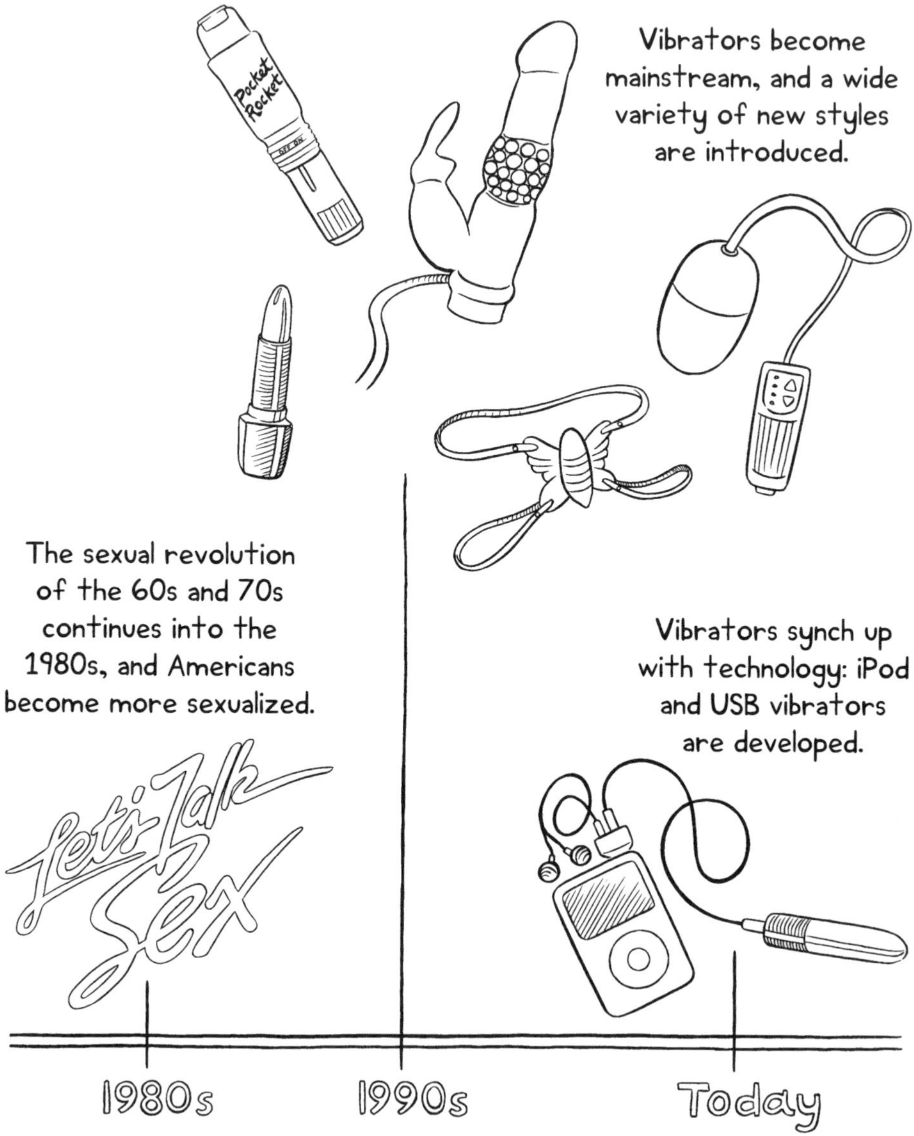
Pocket Rocket
Vibrators become mainstream, and a wide variety of new styles are introduced.
The sexual revolution of the 60s and 70s continues into the 1980s, and Americans become more sexualized.
Let's Talk Sex
Vibrators synch up with technology: iPod and USB vibrators are developed.
1980s
1990s
Today

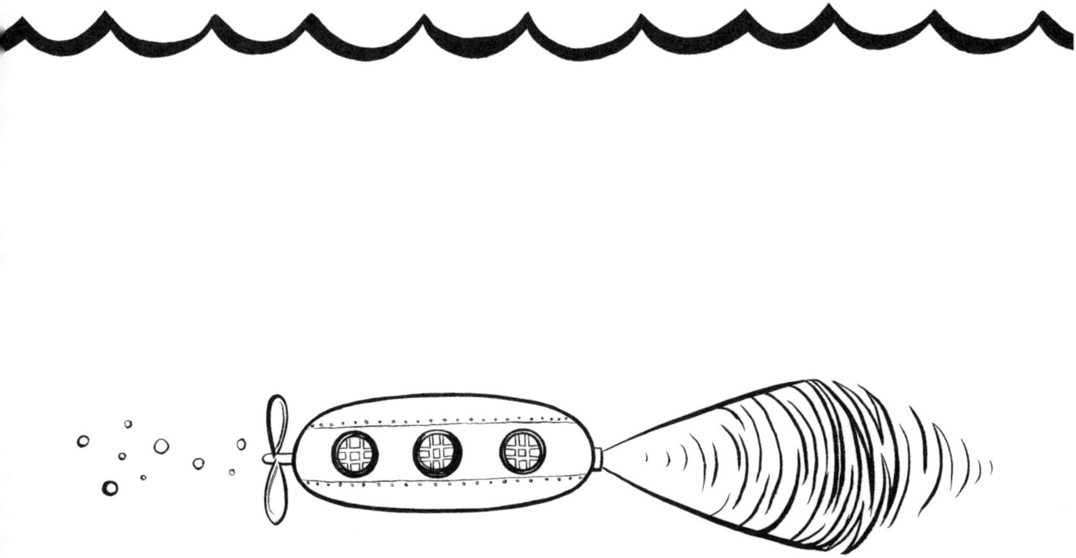

FURTHER STUDIES

sources & resources

BOOKS

A NEW VIEW OF A WOMAN'S BODY, The Federation of Feminist Women's Health Centers, 1991.

OUR BODIES, OURSELVES, The Boston Women's Health Book Collective, 2005.

THE V BOOK: A DOCTOR'S GUIDE TO COMPLETE VULVO-VAGINAL HEALTH, Elizabeth G. Stewart, M.D. and Paula Spencer, 2002.

THE TECHNOLOGY OF ORGASM: "HYSTERIA," THE VIBRATOR, AND WOMEN'S SEXUAL SATISFACTION, Rachel P. Maines, 1999.

MAKING SEX: BODY AND GENDER FROM THE GREEKS TO FREUD, Thomas Laqueur, 1992.

THE G SPOT: AND OTHER DISCOVERIES ABOUT HUMAN SEXUALITY, Alice Kahn Ladas, Beverly Whipple, and John D. Perry, 2005.

SHE COMES FIRST: THE THINKING MAN'S GUIDE TO PLEASURING A WOMAN, Ian Kerner, 2004.

BONK: THE CURIOUS COUPLING OF SCIENCE AND SEX, Mary Roach, 2008.

THE CLITORAL TRUTH: THE SECRET WORLD AT YOUR FINGERTIPS, Rebecca Chalker, 2000.

THE STORY OF V: OPENING PANDORA'S BOX, Catherine Blackledge, 2003.

CAMBODIAN GRRRL: SELF-PUBLISHING IN PHNOM PENH, Anne Elizabeth Moore, 2011.

FILM

ORGASM INC.: THE STRANGE SCIENCE OF FEMALE PLEASURE, Liz Canner, 2009 (www.orgasminc.org).

ARTICLES

"EXPOSED AT LAST: THE TRUTH ABOUT YOUR CLITORIS," Jennifer Johnson, *Women's Health: Readings on Social, Economic, and Political Issues*, Kendall Hunt Publishing Company, 2004.

"THE INTERNAL CLITORIS," Ms. M, *Museum of Sex Blog*, November 30, 2011.

"SEX ON THE BRAIN: WHAT TURNS WOMEN ON, MAPPED OUT," Linda Geddes, *New Scientist*, August 5, 2011.

"WHY WE REALLY NEED TO GET OVER THE G-SPOT," Elizabeth Black, *Alternet*, February 11, 2010.m

"WHY EVERYBODY'S WRONG ABOUT THE G-SPOT," Jamie Condliffe, *Gizmodo*, April 25, 2012.

(in response to:)

"G-SPOT ANATOMY: A NEW DISCOVERY," Dr. Adam Ostrzenski, Journal of Sexual Medicine, 2012.

WEB

THE INTERNAL CLITORIS (video), Betty Dodson, *YouTube*, October 15, 2007 > youtube.com/watch?v=BIbbZ37A7RQ

SCARLETEEN.COM (Sex Ed for the Real World)
> scarleteen.com

SEX, ETC. (Sex Education Magazine & Website by and for Teens) > sexetc.org

GO ASK ALICE (Columbia University's Health Q&A)
> goaskalice.columbia.edu

OUR BODIES, OURSELVES (Women's Health and Sexuality)
> ourbodiesourselves.org

PSYCHOLOGICAL HISTORY OF WOMEN
> psychistofwomen.umwblogs.org

WIKIPEDIA
>> urethral sponge, skene's gland, female ejaculation, g-spot, vibrator, orgasm, one sex two sex theory.

PERFORMING LIVE AT THE CLITORIS!